Swallowing the Stem of Adam's Apple

Swallowing the Stem of Adam's Apple
Copyright © 2021 Laura Kiesel

All Rights Reserved.
Printed in the United States of America.
First Edition, 2021.
Published by Unsolicited Press.
ISBN: 978-1-950730-72-8

No part of this book may be used or reproduced in any manner whatsoever without written permission except in the case of brief quotations embodied in critical articles or reviews.

Unsolicited Press
Portland, Oregon
www.unsolicitedpress.com
orders@unsolicitedpress.com
619-354-8005

Cover Design: Kathryn Gerhardt
Editor: S.R. Stewart

Swallowing the Stem of Adam's Apple

By Laura Kiesel

Acknowledgements

I would like to thank the following journals for their publication of my individual poems:

Upstreet and *Blue Lake Review*: "Stem"

Medulla Review: "RED" and "Rhythmless"

Fox Chase Review: "Hair"

Amethyst Arsenic: "Clam Poem" and "Conversation with my Pen"

Ibbetson Street: "Wish for an Aspiring Herpetologist"

Noctua Review: "Music"

Stone Highway Review: "October" and "Fever Dreams"

Naugatuck River Review: "What Tea Can't Cure"

Wilderness House Literary Review: "A Poem for Uncle," "Nature," and "The Mercy of Eyelids"

Gin Bender: "For My Mother" and "Devils"

Poems

Rhythmless	7
Fever Dreams	9
Devils	10
Conversation with My Pen	12
RED	13
Clam Poem	17
Nature	19
For My Mother	21
October	24
Ghosts	25
Hair	28
Rust	30
Wish for an Aspiring Herpetologist	32
A Poem for Uncle	34
What Tea Can't Cure	35
The Mercy of Eyelids	37
Some Nights	39
Primitive	41
Stem	42
Music	44
About the Author	47
About the Press	48

Rhythmless

She goes chained to the tremor of a rhythm that never arrives.
—Frederico García Lorca ("The Passage of the Siguiriya")

We have considered want, to be in its bondage.
But to rhythm is another thing.

I've imagined feet soles shoe-laced with cymbals, a mouth smiling
        piano-key teeth.
Violin-stringed sinews.

The skies stretched out with sheet music, with music symbols floating
        around like snowflakes adrift, to
reach past the town limits to where the city turns gritty and the ground is
        strewn with syringes.

Morning brings its own music: the sound of spoons clanging against
        coffee cups, the teakettle's whistle,
the whispers of grandparents against the backdrop of static-lined weather
        reports.

But what if the bondage was waiting for the want?

The dawn that brings no birdsong.

In the city, the skyscrapers may scream their white noise, the traffic jams
        bullying people into the day's
end with brisk backslaps till they reach the gutter and bottom out.

But later on there will be a moon, shining its halo on the dark wingtips of
        black butterflies that flutter

manically through the mist of this balmy midnight.

Here a woman walks, her bare feet moistened by a mossy path. Chains
          hug her waist and breasts like
large bracelets, and are wound into her braided hair. The blade in her
          hand can't cut through the chains,
but chafes her wrists and glows against the fountains.

She expects to hear some score to her drama, an uprush of symphony to
          announce her as the serpents
slide in. But it doesn't come, and even the advancing snakes are silent,
          their famished tongues flickering
stoically.

Flowers spoon limes and swallow their wedges, spraying citrus on her
          smock.

Oleander petals fall, as mute as swans.

Fever Dreams

As a child, I suffered frequently from fevers.
Laid up on the living room couch, with a cold cloth on my forehead
I watched Disney movies and other fantasy films.

When I slept, these characters flooded my dreams
 where they grew fangs and became less cute.

Their bite marks itched me like the hives that sprang up spontaneously on
        my skin in erratic
polka dot patterns, itched me like the chicken pox I got not once but
        twice in third grade,
some now scratched to ragged scars on my skinny shoulders.

As young as six, my dreams were tinged with sex:
Cinderella being pawed by Snow White's seven dwarves,
Dorothy's dalliances with Scarecrow and Tin Man.

To put the fire out, I was tossed sobbing into tubs of ice water my
        stepfather's hand firmly pressing my
head under as if for the final baptism, as if the first blessing in my infancy
        was not, and would have
never been, enough.

When I awoke sometime later in the melting mock igloo, the air steaming
        and my hair sizzling like wet
electricity, the scorched muscle in my mouth was always still too swollen
to allow me to either shut my mouth or scream.

Devils

I know not what I do
when I have taken to this ugly habit
of sleeping at night.

Sins are salty,
and need to be sweated out slowly.

And I have closed the corpses in the closet,
ate bees to sting my mouth swollen
so maybe I would learn silence.

When I was young, my brother and I
traced words on each other's backs,
guessing at the words,
(Naughty Words)
while my mother fought her devils in the kitchen.

Devils, yes they exist,
with their hard-wrought, wrinkled hands,
fashioned to hold some firm ball of weight,
that piece of you that is your core
and stretch it as thin and transparent
as raw egg white.

I hoped I wouldn't have my own (devils, that is).
But one day they came firmly red like the lick of a flame
and burnt my backside.

They came and made me put on my shoes
no matter how sleepy
no matter how heartsick
So I could sit in a corner somewhere conspicuous
With empty wine and whiskey glasses
and obsolete wishes crumpled in my back pocket.

What could make me look in an empty alleyway
for affection.

What could make me stick my hand into fire even when
I have already lost so much skin.

My mother sometimes shrieked,
ripped the sleeves off of her sweat-soaked shirts.

She sometimes thought I was a devil and split my lips
with her fists.

I don't make much noise though, when they visit me.

I absorb them with sponge-like accuracy.
I tremble and swallow my tongue.
I sometimes even bend over to oblige them
and get it over with quickly.

Conversation with My Pen

I can no longer do with your sullen silence, a propped up phallus with no target, the monument pointing to the void of an empty page, occasionally leaking your ink prematurely, spoiling what could be a poem.
I would like you to reclaim your throne, thrill you to again take me by the hand. What you made was always so much lovelier: a graceful dance of arabesques, an origami of words taking the shapes of songbirds and sailboats. You gave my words curves, curling them into ringlets until they charmed like a dozen tap dancing Shirley Temples.

A poem written by a pen is one smoking a cigarette, drinking a martini. A poem written by a pen is one wearing a short skirt while crossing and uncrossing its legs. It is all cleavage and no concealment, while the laptop poem is a pin-stripe pantsuit, black coffee, black tie affair. It's all formal with no frills or fragility, whereas the handwritten poem twists and writhes and sinks its jagged edges into x's and scribbles.

With the keyboard poem, any error is erased by the backspace button, showing no traces of the traveled road, all crumbs left along the way eaten eagerly by a machine until all that's left is the perfect poem.

Because you see, the laptop is like the vibrator you buy to keep up with the quickness of your needs, whereas the pen is the hand you used before technology intervened. You know which way is faster, but also which way bends best with your body, giving you the long and satisfying moan instead of just a quick gasp and spasm.

RED

I.

It came with the howls that sliced through the night like a knife—a blood stained blade that broke the dam in my belly, releasing rivers of red (the color of my cloak) from between my trembling thighs. The moon was full that night—it glared like a gold coin, partially shrouded by dark clouds that seemed to scratch at its copper face.

My mother, alarmed, thought me too young for this affliction, though I was advancing on my sixteenth year. Adhering to her admonishments, I kept clean as best I could, though the stubborn blood flooded instead of spotted, soaking my skirts and scarring my bed sheets while I slept.

I was warned against going into the woods at this time—that it would bring the wild things to come sniffing up my skirt, making them drool more than any meat or bread in my basket would. They would lap me clean and then hard, till I'd be nothing but bone.

I knew my mother didn't only mean the wolves, but the woodsmen wielding their axes, the ones who butchered the trees every October, leaving a trail of twigs piercing the path that led straight to their modest huts. These men hummed instead of howled, but it sent the same shudder down my spine, leading me to follow the somber sound through the woods to their working groups encircled by the scent of wood smoke and musk.

There is one woodsman whose hair and beard are as red as the small death I shed each month. When he hums, the wild howls in the woods stutter and then briefly cease. But when they start up again, they entwine with his hum, emerging as a mutual melody so that I can't discern the difference between those beasts and this man....

II.

One day, months later, when the cramps come kicking my belly with unusual belligerence, the blood running redder and hotter than fire, I am solicited for an urgent errand. Equipped with a crucifix and a basket full of fresh milk and fruit preserves, I am sent to aid my ailing grandmother. I depart at dusk. Before leaving for my mission, my mother bathed me, rubbed my thighs with mint leaves to mask my scent, inserted a makeshift plug to barricade the blood that wailed in my womb for its freedom. I am told to keep my eyes alert but also averted, to stay off shadowed paths. I am also commanded to keep my cloak at home, because the red will draw wolves. But in secret, I hid it in my basket beneath the food, freeing it and fastening it over my body once I was at the forest's edge...

So I go swiftly, my long white arms slicing the wind, the nape of my neck matted with the dark hairs strays the sweat has planted there. Ignoring instructions, I run, though I was warned this would make me be perceived as prey. Suddenly, behind me I hear a cascade of crunching noises, dry leaves crushed under a dozen leaping paws. Then comes the howling.

It starts with a single low baritone moan, but others join in and it rises in concert to a pitch reached by the highest notes of a string symphony. The moon shivers to the tune, as does my body. I shake so hard as I run among shadows, that the blood bursts free from its barricade. Red runs down my legs and heavily flecks the forest floor in my wake...

III.

I do not remember the final fall, just the corner of my cloak catching a low tree branch that sent me tumbling, trailing the blood behind me like bread crumbs for the creatures following at my ankles. When I wake, I don't hear howls, only a humming. I lie on a wood floor in front of a fire. Besides the cloak draped over my damp body, I am naked. The crimson flow continues, absorbed by the cloak that shares its color. When I stand I see him watching me: red hair and beard framing feral eyes. They dart out of the shadows and consume me. I know now: he will lap me bone clean. I should feel fear, but I don't.

IV.

There are barely any things that are redder, wetter than blood. But there are sounds that shout deeper blushes than what my body can make. There are lips and tongues, deep caverns that hold quivering secrets that can only be expelled when shared. When this happens, the first flowers find the strength to smash through the snow and announce spring. When this happens, the rush of blood slows down to hardly a trickle, calmed at last by a worthy diversion.

V.

Later on, I am led the way out of the woods by wolves. They caress my cleaned skirts with their snouts, nuzzle my palms, licking my fingers free of fruit jam. No more monsters than the moon or woods, they whimper plaintively for my approval. When we reach the hill overlooking home, I plan to go forward but instead find a furred collar in my grip. I let it lead me away, to caves where the colors I create will be welcomed, where there are no mothers with clucking tongues.

The woods pull me in, keep me secret, so that all that remains of me is the blood-stained cloak I abandoned on the forest floor, and the memory of me as told by the townspeople, who continue to whisper of wolves and their hunger.

Clam Poem

Love, the heart is a clam that can make pearls out of sand.

You itched me, inched deep into the soft pink flesh of my heart.
At each turn, I sweated and coated you, until you built to my resistance.

Marble-smooth and perfect, you were there nestled deep inside, where it
        was warm,
Not feeling the effects of saltwater that stung my shell with its intentions.
Flare-ups in my eyes and lips, only so many leaks could I spring before
Breathing became difficult, until I drowned...

I tried to spit you out.
But further you burrowed, until a hole formed under my tongue where the
        major vein lives.
Until an indent swelled in the raw pit of my pelvis.

You hibernated there, caught up in the canyon of my impervious shell,
        shocked into submission.
Further subdued under skin you mistook for satin sheets, you were
        pristine,
Baptized by the holy water of my saliva.

I let you live and made you a jewel, a virgin gem.
I shut myself around you, a closed fist, frightened by outsiders and ready
        to fight for your
Defense, eager to keep my treasure.

A beast with the beauty inside, I ingested you. Not fully, though:
I kept you there on back of my tongue.
Testing your taste, letting you linger.

You outlived me.
Smaller but brighter, you went on to better hands and harder flesh.
You see the sun now while I am to be another's meal.

Love, the heart is like a clam
That snaps shut at intrusion.

Nature

The beast that uses its belly to crawl, forked-tongue tasting air for hints
        of flesh,
be it baby or not...

We have put our sins on him—
spat out the apple slices and tucked our own sins in the artificial skins of
        clothes,
keeping our fingernails clean when consuming our pre-packaged meat.

And then there is breakfast—
the smooth suppleness of an egg cradles the sun center of life.
Sometimes when you crack it, there are drops of blood.

It begs the question: is it food or family?

The Rhesus monkey with its mechanical mother, the dry breast,
 the furry fingers wrenched arthritic in the terry-cloth cover,
gripping for the heartbeat, heartsick to crawl into the crux
        of the gene machine,
to be cradled in authentic arms.

Nature or nurture is the eternal argument.

Does that change whether the costume be
Scales or skin?
Feathers or fur?

And what about survival?

When a final screech is emitted in a flurry of bloody, dispersed feathers,
It reminds us all that even a nest can become a noose.

For My Mother

lips that would kiss form prayers of broken stone
—T.S. Eliot ("The Hollow Men")

You, whose sullen cheeks
set deep in a smile-less face,
mindlessly miming the chores of motherhood…

Oh Hail Marys
Oh Our Fathers

Acts of Contrition
enacted, contrived
your forearm a host
to razorblade and syringe wounds
veins ready to break open
and flood our kitchen with blood.

I found my own form
in the mirror
in my shadow-dark bedroom and fathomed
our faces were the same
but my brows were thicker
so that maybe meant
we were different.

And you taught me
God's word while

picking the prick
from your leg.

(Lifeless
 sometimes I lie at night,
 my childhood lullabies
still swooning in my head—all lies.)
You pecked my forehead

Faintly,
pale lips that stuck like paste
that sometimes smacked my face
with hard words.

(Older now,
and I have no one
My mouth is
Lonely.)

I wrenched my fingers free from this wheel
And learned my own words
Words, husky and wet
to trance me
treat me harshly
sing me sour-soft to sleep.

My lips split open like a wound
words bleed and congeal...

Were those words "mother"?
"God"?

Or just some stones I spat out?

October

This month is the mourning veil.

As sky and poppies bleed,
we take our tired hands to pick the harvest.
Fingers full of fruit pulp, the sticky stems strangle our bare wrists
and scream *murder*.

We lick ourselves clean
debase our food with ghoulish faces while we dress down
as ghosts or monsters.

Make us something else we scream,
sear our flesh and strip us down to bone.
We're suffocating in our skins, you see,
in our buckles and blue jeans and dirty black boots.
We're invisible in our human uniforms
and so go singing down the streets,
soliciting sweets and smiles from strangers.

What else could we do but pluck live things
from the ground we will all one day be buried dead in?

What else but play gods and monsters for a day,
and put up shields of bright orange to deflect
the foreboding gray?

Ghosts

She didn't understand that I've seen ghosts, coming up crazed from her
        current coke fix and needing
another chemo session.

I've seen her ovaries on the sonogram screen: not ripe oranges, but
video game villains. A cartoon—this coked out body I came from,
choking on the next line, finding the next free vein on the interstate
        highway
right before radiation treatment.

I felt nothing. Even matches self-inflicted on the skin left no sting.

My mind wanted a mother gone, but she was acquitted—
black-lunged bitch who birthed this bleeding liberal-hearted girl whose
        bloated face
had less color than the hospital walls.

I wailed some nights, limbs flailing like a fish flopping on land.
"I am possessed," I said. "I see ghosts. Satan lives inside me."

You all stared squarely at me and scoffed at my suicidal rants.
But we took the Bible off the bookshelf; crucifixes came down from the
        walls to hide in
dresser drawers all through my high school years.

Catholicism promises Christ comes to the faithful.
But I dreamed of demons and blood, black holes in the ground
        swallowing me whole.

Even my freckles were pale dirt stains set against the paler surface of my
    skin.
I slept through adolescence and the anger cracked and peeled my skin.

"Fire freezes me," I said on some nights when the fevers brought hives
    and hiccups,
3am crying jags and sharp sugar cravings with sunrise.

Summer was the worst.

Sometimes the sun bled against the sky and it spilled over and stained me:
blood-red brick walls, blood running out from between my legs,
a broken faucet, cramps bending me, curved like a fetus, crying to be a
    boy instead.
And the water: never-running, a never-ending drought, the fire hydrants
    outside stealing our supply. A
dead dog lying on the living room floor, dehydrated. A dead uncle in the
    next room, belly-up, belly-full of
pills.

Forget the past.
Pin-up the teen idol posters, pin up the memories others pretend I should
    have.

I remember she threw the Christmas tree down the stairs when the heroin
    was gone,
kicked my stomach to sooth her own crazy ache.

I stuck my fingernails into my palms till poke-tricks of blood peeked out,
bit my bottom lip to keep the screams inside.

I swore the sky would sing for me one day, the marks leaving only faded
    scars.
I feel safer with the crucifixes down and the Bible off the bookshelf,
the demons just a distant dream.

"I still see ghosts sometimes" I tell no one but myself, "faded to that
    sliver of moonlight that hits my face
some nights from the window near my bed."

But I know the ghosts will be gone when I stop leaving dead things on my
    doorstep.

Hair

Somewhat like a strand of hair gone gray, I attempt
to rip you out right at the root

Astonished by the sudden shock of opaque,
I gape at the white line, the white sign,
that tells me something sick is penetrating the shaft.
Like a skunk stripe branding my skull.
(Is it my skull or soul I rip you from?)

And is it just a single strand, or the symptom
of many to come invading, until my head stands—a canyon of
        colorlessness?
A field of gray grass aghast against the white winter?

I itch.
Could it be dandruff?
Or the snowflakes swooning down from the sky and caught in my tangled
        mass of hair
like netted butterflies?
I scratch until the skin sloughs off and the bone beneath bleeds.
At least blood puts some color in my braid.

Every weed I pluck out produces two more in its place,
until I've been bleached, the brown and burgundy shades replaced by
signs of premature age.

I have been blotted out by your betrayal.
As all my pastels go pale

the hues and blues of my mood cinder to a cool ice cube void of color.

My fingers beg for baldness
and trichotillomania takes over.

Each yank is like its own small surgery,
a tumor taken out, the shoot of the chemo syringe up the tender vein.
Each pull is the whip against my Puritan skin.

Once a Rapunzel in the making,
sloping her hair down the tower, entreating
you to climb, a shining head of hair, thick-carpeted and fine.

I have severed the staircase, step by step and strand by strand.

Once I had a mane of glory.
Now I wear a wig.

Rust

We don't like rust, it reminds us that we are dying
—Brett Singer

Sleep scoured from a metal pot of memory, while the loose twang of
    twilight fills the room…

All night long, there is the thought of your disease,
flitting like an insect along the periphery of your dreams.

We are chewed up creatures who need machines to live,
our bowels black snakes ready to unravel out of our bodies.

At the bar, you offered your liver to it.
Others I've known (at other times and places) their blood, breasts, and
    breath.

You dared me once to lick rust: run my tongue along the grooves of an
    old nail, to taste its decay. You
said it would help me understand death better, more than eating meat or
hanging out in hospital waiting rooms.

Later, I told you we were like trees, huddled close together but never
    touching,
collecting the seasons, the only parts of ourselves that overlap
the shadows we cast at the end of the day
or the pieces we shed when late fall's brittle winds blow through us.

Every leaf, even an evergreen's needle, is determined to die:
fall from its once suspended height to be trampled under the boots and
        hooves of others.

This is what it is, that dermal layer that coats the forest floor (and
        eventually us all)
in the colors of rust.

Wish for an Aspiring Herpetologist

Though the tumor was tiny,
it didn't stop the cancer from quickly speckling your lymph nodes
like the freckled spots found on an otherwise
even-colored egg.

In my dreams, your fingers fall off like flower petals;

your lips and teeth collapse, smothering your mouth so that you can't call
        to me.
I watch you wither, and when I go to grab your hands, it is my own
        fingertips that curl and
crumble like burning paper.

In the pictures I have of you, you chase tree frogs through the forest,
a spotted salamander slinks up your skirt. You smiled and called this a
        cute flirtation--you who
cooed to snakes as though they were kittens,

letting them coil around your outstretched arms like lace.

Neither of us knew breasts could become malignant before thirty.
The rumor is that while they are still taut, they can't turn against you.
But now, instead of your impending marriage, mortality is on your mind,
your next exam will not be for school, but to gauge your bones
for further signs of the sickness.

But here's a secret: in winter, frogs don't fully freeze.
Their blood slows but doesn't stop, as they sleep with their souls on hold,
breathless in the bottoms of ice ponds, awaiting spring.

Each blood cell they possess is a small miracle because it doesn't burst,
but has learned to trick not only cold, but death.

I wish the same for you: a long slumber from the cold pain of your cancer,
from which you will awake to the healing blush of the sun.
When you do, you will erupt an armor of scales, sprout new limbs and
        flee back into the forest,
like a lizard newly hatched and hungry for the dawn.

A Poem for Uncle

The inseam of uncle's jacket
matches the inseam of his coffin:
satin, periwinkle-purple…such soft words,
such softness inside the dense wood,
like some tough fruit, a pineapple perhaps,
its skin callused hard and impervious around its mushy pulp.

When the heat permeates the ground, it lasers through the oak-wood,
sears the skin and pits out the rot, like when we eat Concord Grapes,
our teeth splitting the skin from the flavor.

Is that what the worms do?
Eat through the sins and leave the seeds for God?
The bones left there idly planted in the ground to grow trees
and believers?

My uncle's baby fine hair, combed over the bald spot.
Covering up the bad spot.

We bury the bad things.
We leave the worms to seed out the secrets, the bare bones,
and leave them there for God.

We, we can't see that much, we need to keep them covert.
In a coffin.
We need some spirit guide to bear it away and
so dig it deep inside the swelter of Earth.

What Tea Can't Cure

To you, tea was the cure-all for any trouble.

Weighed down with milk and white sugar, it coated our throats with
        warmth,
making us speak only sweetness, our eyes luminous with love.

But at night, clumsy fingers fumbled the lids off pill bottles, secrets
        stashed
in the backs of cigarette packs.

Tobacco smoke was safe you said, but bracing a bare foot for contact
with a cold floor tile, or leaving home with a wet head in winter,
was not something to be dared. Such carelessness causes coughing,
spurs the lungs to fill with fluid the way wood streams gorge in spring
after the last of the snow melts.

Years later, dark flecks would collect inside your chest—
a flock of blackbirds beating their rusty wings
against arthritic rib bones, a sickness the color of cobwebs,
                eating your flesh from where you inhale.

They sent you home with an oxygen tank we were warned
could cause combustion if even the smallest flicker of fire
lit up your face.

So stubborn were you at the thought of a life without smoking, that you
        set about to die.

Within weeks you were a woman of wires,
which kept you barely breathing and alive,
a network of cylinders that sucked like leeches at your opened orifices.

In the hospital, your hands swallowed by white mittens
the size and shape of boxing gloves, Velcroed tight at the wrist to keep
you from clawing your way to the final freedom,
draining you of your remaining dignity when you tried to touch my face,
rounded glove-tip bouncing gently off my cheek like a marshmallow.

You were itchy, I could see, so I scratched--your neck and face,
as I did for my cat when he came home with a plastic collar after surgery
to keep him from licking his wounds raw.

When the nurses left, I took a glove off and we held hands as your eyes
	closed.
I watched you sleep for the last time, my courtesy tea untouched on the
	table,
losing its heat with each passing second.

The Mercy of Eyelids

Sleep was sacrament my body always craved: to fall face down into
    fluffed-up pillows, to slip into a small
coma that would erase the oppressive hours when the sun is too high and
    glares too hard and you crave
dusk like a warm drink.

When my eyesight becomes blurry from my dried-out contact lenses, I
    close my eyes and let the tears
flush out the dust, but when I open them, it's all too clear: vibrant colors
    smacking my eyes at every angle
so sleep again becomes a welcome thought.

And then there was you, suddenly all puffed up on the love I handfed you
    as though you were a prized
parrot or portly king.

And everything I gave you returned ten-fold: you thought of me every
    minute of every day you said, and
I, finally finding a home in someone else's thoughts, found I could sleep
    again.

It was the sense of homelessness that kept my quaking body always awake,
    the untethered sensation
only orphans can know, with no parents to teach them prayers or tuck
    them in.

It was as if my eyes had now become yours, and because I could be so
`much kinder to you than to myself,

I let them close and settle into sleep, showed them the mercy I knew
    you'd bestow on them if you
could—the mercy of eyelids.

Some Nights

There are some nights when I want nothing more than to shut this soft
        heart like a fist.
To fix it, fit it, into some stone-thick substance, so that the fruit of it
        stays frozen and unable to ferment.
A fossil.

I have tried to scoop out its suppleness, the little bursts of extricated
        flavor that stick to the skin and
begin to stink to high heaven.

Can you feel it folding over and into itself like a sleeping lover?

Blanketed, but not dormant—you swept your hands down the sides and
        the layers would slink down like
sleeping eyelids, but when you peeled them back up and off, didn't it
        prick your pretty eyes with its
pungency, making you cry?

I have even put pillowcases over the peach-shaped creature breathing
        behind my breastbone, hoping it
would stop kicking me like a hungry child of the womb, thumping me
        with its rabbit feet until I fake
submission or sleep.

I cannot evade it.

Both like a clock ticking and thunder clouds clapping, it whispers and
        screams at the same time the way

only a great poem or painting can. It won't shut up.

I want to hold it hard in my hand, so that it is a shell with some kind of
        hermit crab inside, wincing with
its pincers poised, ready to puncture the prying eyes of trespassers

Instead of the creature you've held.

The way your fingers slipped into it like it was an overripe tomato you
        tested for firmness
that failed. You knuckle-deep in the acrid red of it, the dermal layer
        dented and decaying in your iron
 grasp.

And what's inside of it seeps into the rest of me and stains my milky
        bones,
making them malleable, soft eels swimming against the contours of my
        flesh.
I lay down at night and wish for the opposite: for my heart to become
        bone—
virgin, cold and hard.

Primitive

There is always the part of us that wants to be primitive: to suck raw meat
        from an animal's marrow, to
stare at fire and really believe a god inhabits the flame...

When we walked into the woods, even the trees trembled, noises sounded
        around us we couldn't ascribe
to anything, not the screech owls or rustling leaves, when we realized they
        were coming from us: our old
war cries.

When we came home, we stripped off civilization as though it were our
        work clothes, till nothing lay on
our bodies but our bare skin.

We could no longer pretend there was a poetry to our politics, a music to
        the monotony of our daily
routines.

Leaving behind everything but our basest desires, we climbed into bed and
        clung to each other like
the kind of creatures that dwell in caves, quivering the way our ancient
        ancestors must have, forgetting their
fears every night as they emptied themselves into each other's dark, damp
        bodies.

Stem

I would love to feed you
Heaping Spoonfuls
of words, frothy with sin(cerity)
and watch your Adam's apple
jut **up** and down
with the ingestion.

And would you please, then,
take me by the hips
still hungry
coercing couplets
in your need
take sensuous sips
till your belly bloated
with my sweetness.

And when it is done
I want a serpent-moment
our forked-tongues
splitting rivers
into streams
into trickles
of timepieces
then tongue-tied
the subsequent silence
still articulate.

And to seal it
I want to remain naked
as rebellion against
the god of shame
proving we not only
ate the flesh of Adam's apple
but also swallowed the stem.

Music

It is all summed up by the things we miss:

The sweat soaked up by our balled-up shirts in summertime, the seats of
    cars that smell of
cigarette smoke and barbecues, the rumble of an engine as the automobile
    peals up the New York State Thruway
and transforms into the Mass Pike, giving way to mountain ranges and
    raw cadences of sky ripped apart
by violent sunsets that bleed into the concrete.

It is the growling in my groin as it reverberates with the rock lyrics on the
    radio and my hair snarled
around the bedpost in my lover's bedroom, or flattened by his palms in
    loose strands against the sheets.

It was once a habit of mine to run in the rain. The beads of water slipped
    down my skin till I felt like a
vertical fish that had exchanged gills for ears. I prayed for rain. Dreamed
    of it...rain and music, some
whiskey to warm the bowl of my belly, or a cold beer to press against my
    temples and cool my flushed
face after a day spent swimming, the twitch of my fingertips typing, or
    sprawling across the paper,
spilling a cascade of crooked calligraphy to stain tattered notebooks and
    bar napkins.

It is the slow swaying of hips, the stone-hard sureness of bones. It is a
    becoming, a perpetual state of

becoming—birth and blood sewn into the indexes of guitar strings and
        piano keys, thunder becoming a
drum beat, a drum beat a heartbeat…the horns and harmonicas that
        scream
and squeal at a pitch higher than, but in the same context, as our human
        voices.

If I could sing, I would open my mouth now and let loose the banshee
        wail my body knows as it recalls
the memory of my birth and becoming, and the rapture of redemption.

About the Author

Laura Kiesel is a widely published journalist, essayist and poet. Her articles and essays have appeared in *The Atlantic, The Guardian, Politico, Vice, Salon, the Washington Post, Al-Jazeera America* and many others. Her poems have been featured in u*pstreet, Medulla Review, Fox Chase Review, Stone Highway Review, Noctua Review, Amethyst Arsenic, Naugatuck River Review, Ibbetson Street* and more. Originally from Brooklyn, New York, she currently resides in the Boston area, where she works as a freelance writer and editor and is part of the teaching faculty at Grub Street.

About the Press

Unsolicited Press was founded in 2012 and is based in Portland, Oregon. The small press publishes fiction, poetry, and creative nonfiction written by award-winning and emerging authors.

Learn more at www.unsolicitedpress.com.

www.ingramcontent.com/pod-product-compliance
Lightning Source LLC
Chambersburg PA
CBHW030141100526
44592CB00011B/985